JOURNAL

52-Week Devotional *for* Christian Women

The 4 Pillars of Growth

By
JOSEPHINE THOMAS

Kingdom Assignment for Christian Women

Draw Me Closer: The Four Pillars of Growth — Journal
52-Week Devotional for Christian Women

2025 Josephine Thomas. All rights reserved.

Published by Pure and Unblemished Limited

ISBN: 979-8-9921054-6-9

All Scriptures are from the New Living Translation Bible unless otherwise stated.

Scripture quotations are taken from the Holy Bible, New Living Translation, copyright © 1996, 2004, 2015 by Tyndale House Foundation. Used by permission of Tyndale House Publishers, Inc., Carol Stream, Illinois 60188. All rights reserved.

All rights reserved under International Copyright Laws.

No part of this book may be reproduced, stored in a retrieval system or transmitted by any means without the author's written permission.

Cover design and formatting @ 2025 by Kelly Williams Hale

God is with you in
the Sacred Place.

Entering the Sacred Place

How to Use This Journal

The reader will use this 52-week devotional journal alongside the 52-week devotional book. When entering the Sacred Place, you must find a space away from others and distractions. Try to be consistent and find a practical time that works for you daily. Begin by giving thanksgiving to God or worshiping. During this time, remind yourself whom you are drawing near to. Then, quiet your mind as you engage in the weekly session.

Take your time to meditate with the scripture. Reflect on it. Return to the *Woman of God* message in the devotional book. Participate with the reflection questions. Talk with God during this time and allow Him to minister to you as you journal your revelations.

At the end of the 52 weeks, you can reflect on the revelations you received from the Lord. You will have a record of the changes—and growth—you experienced on your journey.

Remember, God is with you in the Sacred Place.

Blessings,
Josephine Thomas
Author and Fellow Woman of God

Table of Contents

PILLAR ONE: RELATIONSHIP WITH GOD

Week 1	*Creator God*	1
Week 2	*Covenant-Keeping God*	5
Week 3	*Holy, holy, holy*	9
Week 4	*I Am Who I Am*	13
Week 5	*The Messiah Son*	17
Week 6	*The Holy Spirit of God*	21
Week 7	*The Source of Love is God*	25
Week 8	*The Just and Righteous God*	29
Week 9	*The Sovereign God*	33
Week 10	*The Omniscient God*	37
Week 11	*The Immutability of God*	41
Week 12	*The Unfailing Love of God*	45
Week 13	*Shelter of God*	49
Week 14	*God Reigns Forever*	53
Week 15	*None Like You God*	57
Week 16	*Exalt the LORD Our God*	61

PILLAR TWO: SPIRITUAL GROWTH

Week 17	*Face It, You're Chosen*	67
Week 18	*Anointed of God*	71
Week 19	*All Authority*	75
Week 20	*The Scriptures Say*	79
Week 21	*Access to the King*	83
Week 22	*The King Fights and Protects You*	87
Week 23	*The Fear of the LORD*	91
Week 24	*Let Your Roots Grow Deep in the Word*	95
Week 25	*Let Your Faith Arise*	99
Week 26	*Higher Thoughts*	103
Week 27	*Search Your Heart*	107
Week 28	*Draw Closer to Me*	111

PILLAR THREE: PERSONAL GROWTH

Week 29	*Seek Him With All Your Heart*	117
Week 30	*God Knows You*	121
Week 31	*The God Who Sees You*	125
Week 32	*Seasons of Life*	129
Week 33	*Favour of the King*	133
Week 34	*Be Strong and Courageous*	137

Week 35	*Fear Not*	141
Week 36	*Confidence in God*	145
Week 37	*Keep Going*	149
Week 38	*Grateful Heart*	153
Week 39	*Where is Your Trust*	157
Week 40	*Following Jesus*	161

PILLAR FOUR: PURPOSE

Week 41	*Seek God for the Plan*	167
Week 42	*Rahab Believed in the Plan*	171
Week 43	*Hannah's Need Touched God's Need for the Plan*	175
Week 44	*Leah's Heart of Praise for the Plan*	179
Week 45	*Mary's Agreement for the Plan*	183
Week 46	*Naomi and Ruth's Alignment for the Plan*	187
Week 47	*Jesus Fulfilled The Plan of the Father*	191
Week 48	*Bearing Lasting Fruit for the Plan*	195
Week 49	*God Grants Success*	199
Week 50	*God's Plan for Your Life*	203
Week 51	*Testify of the Truth*	207
Week 52	*The Father's Will*	211

Pillar One: Relationship With God

Drawing Closer to God,
Know His Attributes.

*"Intimacy is Born from the Secret Place
Draw Closer to God."*

Week 1

Creator God

Scripture:

> You alone are the LORD. You made the skies and the heavens and all the stars. You made the earth and the seas and everything in them. You preserve them all, and the angels of heaven worship you.
>
> ~ Nehemiah 9:6 NLT

Reflection Questions:

- What amazes or excites you when thinking about God's creation?

_____

_____

_____

_____

_____

Week 1: Creator God

- Do you have childlike awe for your Creator God?

- Do you include yourself when thinking about the splendor of God's creation?

Week 1: Creator God

Revelation From the Sacred Place

Week 2

Covenant-Keeping God

Scripture:

"Now if you will obey me and keep my covenant, you will be my own special treasure from among all the peoples on earth; for all the earth belongs to me. And you will be my kingdom of priests, my holy nation." This is the message you must give the people of Israel.

~ Exodus 19:5-6 NLT

Reflection Questions:

- What are your thoughts on a covenant-keeping God?

_____

_____

_____

_____

_____

Week 2: Covenant Keeping God

- What do you think about your covenant being one of life and not separation?

- How do you feel about all God has done for you?

Week 2: Covenant Keeping God

Revelation From the Sacred Place

Week 3

Holy, holy, holy

Scripture:

Each of these living beings had six wings, and their wings were covered all over with eyes, inside and out. Day after day and night after night, they keep on saying, "Holy, holy, holy is the LORD God, the Almighty—the one who always was, who is, and who is still to come."

~ Revelation 4:8 NLT

Reflection Questions:

- What does God's Holiness mean to you?

_____

_____

_____

_____

_____

Week 3: Holy, Holy, Holy

- Knowing the truth of the Word makes you holy. How is your engagement with the Word?

- What might you do differently to improve your relationship with God?

Week 3: Holy, Holy, Holy

Revelation From the Sacred Place

Week 4

I Am Who I Am

Scripture:

But Moses protested, "If I go to the people of Israel and tell them, 'The God of your ancestors has sent me to you,' they will ask me, 'What is his name?' Then what should I tell them?" God replied to Moses, "I AM WHO I AM. Say this to the people of Israel: I AM has sent me to you."

~ Exodus 3:13-14 NLT

Reflection Questions:

- What does it mean for you to know God's name?

_____

_____

_____

_____

_____

Week 4: I Am Who I Am

- What does your name mean? Does it tell a story about who you are?

- Do you have difficulty talking to God through adversity? How might you change that?

Week 4: I Am Who I Am

Revelation From the Sacred Place

> **Week 5**

The Messiah Son

Scripture:

> *Simon Peter answered, "You are the Messiah, the Son of the living God."*
>
> ~ Matthew 16:16 NLT

Reflection Questions:

- What do you think about the sacrificial love of God for you?

Week 5: The Messiah Son

- Have you called upon the living God today?

- What names signify who God is for you?

Week 5: The Messiah Son

Revelation From the Sacred Place

Week 6

The Holy Spirit of God

Scripture:

*But when the Father sends the Advocate as my representative—
that is, the Holy Spirit—he will teach you everything
and will remind you of everything I have told you.*

~ John 14:26 NLT

Reflection Questions:

- What does your relationship with the Holy Spirit look like?

_____

_____

_____

_____

_____

Week 6: The Holy Spirit of God

- Do you know the Holy Spirit as Comforter or Friend?

- Do you trust the leading of the Holy Spirit?

Week 6: The Holy Spirit of God

Revelation From the Sacred Place

Week 7

The Source of Love is God

Scripture:

We know how much God loves us, and we have put our trust in his love. God is love, and all who live in love live in God, and God lives in them.

~ 1 John 4:16 NLT

Reflection Questions:

- What do you think about when reflecting on God's love?

Week 7: The Source of Love is God

- Have you connected with God's love today?

- Can you bring to God today any area of your life that needs healing and transforming by His love?

Revelation From the Sacred Place

Week 8

The Just and Righteous God

Scripture:

He is the Rock; his deeds are perfect. Everything he does is just and fair. He is a faithful God who does no wrong; how just and upright he is!

~ Deuteronomy 32:4 NLT

Reflection Questions:

- What are your thoughts about God's nature being just and fair?

Week 8: The Just and Righteous God

- Do you recognize God's hand of justice in your life?

- What are your thoughts about championing a cause? Do you have one?

Week 8: The Just and Righteous God

Revelation From the Sacred Place

Week 9

The Sovereign God

Scripture:

*For the LORD your God is the God of gods and Lord of lords.
He is the great God, the mighty and awesome God,
who shows no partiality and cannot be bribed.*

~ Deuteronomy 10:17 NLT

Reflection Questions:

- Have you placed anything above the sovereignty of God?

Week 9: The Sovereign God

- What are your thoughts about God being incorruptible?

- Can you readily take your concerns to God now, knowing He is above all?

Week 9: The Sovereign God

Revelation From the Sacred Place

Week 10

The Omniscient God

Scripture:

Remember the things I have done in the past. For I alone am God! I am God, and there is none like me. Only I can tell you the future before it happens. Everything I plan will come to pass, for I do whatever I wish.

~ Isaiah 46:9-10 NLT

Reflection Questions:

- How often do you lose focus? What helps you re-focus on God?

Week 10: The Omniscient God

- How do you imagine your future?

- Do you reflect on what God has done for you in your life?

Week 10: The Omniscient God

Revelation From the Sacred Place

Week 11

The Immutability of God

Scripture:

> I am the LORD, and I do not change. That is why you descendants of Jacob are not already destroyed.
>
> ~ Malachi 3:6 NLT

Reflection Questions:

- What are your thoughts about the Immutability of God?

Week 11: The Immutability of God

- What promises do you want to keep hold of with this assurance?

- Have you ever considered how the Immutability of God would impact others?

Week 11: The Immutability of God

Revelation From the Sacred Place

Week 12

The Unfailing Love of God

Scripture:

*With your unfailing love you lead the people
you have redeemed. In your might,
you guide them to our sacred home.*

~ Exodus 15:13 NLT

Reflection Questions:

- What are your thoughts on God's unfailing love?

Week 12: The Unfailing Love of God

- Can you recognise that you are loved?

- Can you put your trust in God's love for you?

Week 12: The Unfailing Love of God

Revelation From the Sacred Place

Week 13

Shelter of God

Scripture:

Those who live in the shelter of the Most High will find rest in the shadow of the Almighty. This I declare about the LORD: He alone is my refuge, my place of safety; he is my God, and I trust him. For he will rescue you from every trap and protect you from deadly disease. He will cover you with his feathers. He will shelter you with his wings. His faithful promises are your armour and protection.

~ Psalm 91:1-4 NLT

Reflection Questions:

- What are your thoughts on dwelling in the shadow of Almighty God?

Week 13: Shelter of God

- When did you last run into God's embracing arms? What happened?

_____
_____
_____
_____
_____
_____
_____
_____

- Where do you usually go—or what do you usually do—for refuge?

_____
_____
_____
_____
_____
_____

Week 13: Shelter of God

Revelation From the Sacred Place

Week 14

God Reigns Forever

Scripture:

*You will bring them in and plant them on your own mountain—
the place, O LORD, reserved for your own dwelling, the sanctuary,
O LORD, that your hands have established.
"The LORD will reign for ever and ever!"*

~ Exodus 15:17-18 NLT

Reflection Questions:

- What caught your attention in today's message?

_____

_____

_____

_____

Week 14: God Reigns Forever

- Have you spent time with the truth that the LORD shall reign forever and ever? What does it mean for you?

- What might you do to be planted on God's mountain and established in His ways?

Week 14: God Reigns Forever

Revelation From the Sacred Place

Week 15

None Like You, God

Scripture:

Who is like you among the gods, O LORD—glorious in holiness, awesome in splendour, performing great wonders? You raised your right hand, and the earth swallowed our enemies.

~ Exodus 15:11-12 NLT

Reflection Questions:

- Are you still in awe of who God is and the wonders He performs for you?

Week 15: None Like You, God

- Can you say—with your hand on your heart—that there is, *"none like you, God?"*

- Are you drawing closer to God by knowing and spending time with Him?

Week 15: None Like You, God

Revelation From the Sacred Place

Week 16

Exalt the LORD Our God

Scripture:

Exalt the LORD our God!
Bow low before his feet, for he is holy!

~ Psalm 99:5 NLT

Reflection Questions:

- Are you able to exalt God when meeting others?

Week 16: Exalt the LORD Our God

- How spirited is your exaltation towards God?

- Is exaltation and praise a lifestyle you live? Can it become one?

Revelation From the Sacred Place

Pillar Two: Spiritual Growth

True Fulfillment in the Sacred Place With God, Know Who You Are.

"To Become One With the Divine God."

Week 17

Face It, You're Chosen

Scripture:

But you are not like that, for you are a chosen people. You are royal priests, a holy nation, God's very own possession. As a result, you can show others the goodness of God, for he called you out of the darkness into his wonderful light.

~ 1 Peter 2:9 NLT

Reflection Questions:

- Do you struggle with worldly achievements and values?

Week 17: Face It, You're Chosen

- Do you know your identity in Christ Jesus?

- What are your thoughts on the titles Jesus has given you?

Week 17: Face It, You're Chosen

Revelation From the Sacred Place

Week 18

Anointed of God

Scripture:

*The Spirit of the LORD is upon me, for he has anointed me
to bring Good News to the poor. He has sent me to proclaim
that captives will be released, that the blind will see,
that the oppressed will be set free, and that
the time of the LORD's favour has come.*

~ Luke 4:18-20 NLT

Reflection Questions:

- What are your thoughts about being set apart for God's plan?

Week 18: Anointed of God

- What do you think the plan will entail?

- What are your thoughts about being equipped for a specific task?

Week 18: Anointed of God

Revelation From the Sacred Place

Week 19

All Authority

Scripture:

"Yes," he told them, "I saw Satan fall from heaven like lightening! Look, I have given you authority over all the power of the enemy, and you can walk among snakes and scorpions and crush them. Nothing will injure you."

~ Luke 10:18-19 NLT

Reflection Questions:

- How have the power dynamics of others affected you? How did you cope?

Week 19: All Authority

- Do you walk in the authority and power Jesus gave you?

- Do you see yourself as Jesus sees you—as the head and not the tail?

Week 19: All Authority

Revelation From the Sacred Place

Week 20

The Scriptures Say

Scripture:

But Jesus told him, "No! The Scriptures say, 'People do not live by bread alone, but by every word that comes from the mouth of God.'" Then the devil took him to the holy city, Jerusalem, to the highest point of the Temple, and said, "If you are the Son of God, jump off! For the Scriptures say, 'He will order his angels to protect you. And they will hold you up with their hands so you won't even hurt your foot on a stone.'" Jesus responded, "The Scriptures also say, 'You must not test the LORD your God.'"

~ Matthew 4:4-7 NLT

Reflection Questions:

- When the hardships—or the adversary come—how do you usually respond?

Week 20: The Scriptures Say

- What are your thoughts on the temptation of Jesus?

_____
_____
_____
_____
_____
_____
_____
_____

- What are your thoughts on using the Word to change your life?

_____
_____
_____
_____
_____
_____
_____
_____

Week 20: The Scriptures Say

Revelation From the Sacred Place

Week 21

Access to the King

Scripture:

> Go and gather together all the Jews of Susa and fast for me. Do not eat or drink for three days, night or day. My maids and I will do the same. And then, though it is against the law, I will go in to see the king. If I must die, I must die.'
>
> ~ Esther 4:16 NLT

Reflection Questions:

- How do you feel about having direct access to the King?

Week 21: Access to the King

- When in trouble, do you remember to go directly to the King?

- Are you aware of the benefits of praying and fasting as part of your lifestyle?

Week 21: Access to the King

Revelation From the Sacred Place

Week 22

The King Fights and Protects You

Scripture:

So Shadrach, Meshach, and Abednego, securely tied, fell into the roaring flames. But suddenly Nebuchadnezzar jumped up in amazement and exclaimed to his advisers, "Didn't we tie up three men and throw them into the furnace?" "Yes, Your Majesty, we certainly did," they replied. "Look!" Nebuchadnezzar shouted. "I see four men, unbound, walking around in the fire unharmed! And the fourth looks like a god!"

~ Daniel 3:23-25 NLT

Reflection Questions:

- Do you trust God to be the fourth person in your fire?

Week 22: The King Fights and Protects You

- How protected do you feel knowing God never sleeps or slumbers?

- Do you have the confidence to battle, knowing God is with you?

Week 22: The King Fights and Protects You

Revelation From the Sacred Place

Week 23

The Fear of the LORD

Scripture:

Fear of the LORD is the foundation of wisdom.
Knowledge of The Holy One results in good judgement.

~ Proverbs 9:10 NLT

Reflection Questions:

- What do you think about the fear of the LORD?

Week 23: The Fear of the LORD

- What are your thoughts on Ananias and Sapphira?

- Do you have a healthy reverence and respect for God?

Week 23: The Fear of the LORD

Revelation From the Sacred Place

Week 24

Let Your Roots Grow Deep in the Word

Scripture:

But they delight in the law of the LORD, meditating on it day and night. They are like trees planted along the river-bank, bearing fruit each season. Their leaves never wither, and they prosper in all they do.

~ Psalm 1:2-3 NLT

Reflection Questions:

- When was the last time you delighted in God's word?

_____

_____

_____

Week 24: Let Your Roots Grow Deep in the Word

- What does mediation look like? Will it be part of your life moving forward?

- What do you think your roots look like? What can you do about it?

Week 24: Let Your Roots Grow Deep in the Word

Revelation From the Sacred Place

Week 25

Let Your Faith Arise

Scripture:

While he was still speaking to her, messengers arrived from the home of Jairus, the leader of the synagogue. They told him, "Your daughter is dead. There's no use troubling the Teacher now." But Jesus overheard them and said to Jairus, "Don't be afraid. Just have faith."

~ Mark 5:35-36 NLT

Reflection Questions:

- What happens when your faith gets shaken?

Week 25: Let Your Faith Arise

- How do you reassure yourself to keep persevering in faith?

- What would an unshakable faith look like? What might you do to achieve this?

Week 25: Let Your Faith Arise

Revelation From the Sacred Place

Week 26

Higher Thoughts

Scripture:

"*My thoughts are nothing like your thoughts,*" *says the LORD.* "*And my ways are far beyond anything you could imagine. For just as the heavens are higher than the earth, so are my ways are higher than your ways and my thoughts higher than your thoughts.*"

~ Isaiah 55:8-9 NLT

Reflection Questions:

- What do you think about God's ways being beyond your imagination?

_____

_____

_____

_____

_____

Week 26: Higher Thoughts

- How much time do you spend with the Holy Spirit to know Him?

- How meaningful is your relationship with the Holy Spirit?

Week 26: Higher Thoughts

Revelation From the Sacred Place

Week 27

Search Your Heart

Scripture:

> Before each young woman was taken to the king's bed, she was given the prescribed twelve months of beauty treatment—six months with oil of myrrh, followed by six months with special perfumes and ointments.
>
> ~ Esther 2:12 NLT

Reflection Questions:

- When did you last take yourself away for a pampering spa or an outing with friends?

Week 27: Search Your Heart

- Do you think it's vital to take self-checks regarding your health?

- Do you find it easy to take a break? Can you change this?

Week 27: Search Your Heart

Revelation From the Sacred Place

Week 28

Draw Closer to Me

Scripture:

When you pray, don't be like the hypocrites who love to pray publicly on street corners and in the synagogues where everyone can see them. I tell you the truth, that is all the reward they will ever get. But when you pray, go away by yourself, shut the door behind you, and pray to your Father in private. Then your Father, who sees everything, will reward you.

~ Matthew 6:5-6 NLT

Reflection Questions:

- Have you ever struggled with prayer? How did you change it?

Week 28: Draw Closer to Me

- Do you feel intimately connected to Father God whilst praying?

- Can you maintain your focus without becoming distracted?

Revelation From the Sacred Place

Pillar Three: Personal Growth

Encouragement for Self-Development, Persevere Through the Journey.

"Fortitude for Your Race."

Week 29

Seek Him with All Your Heart

Scripture:

If you look for me wholeheartedly, you will find me.

~ Jeremiah 29:13 NLT

Reflection Questions:

- How did God capture your attention on your first encounter? How was it memorable for you?

Week 29: Seek Him with All Your Heart

- Do you still seek after God with all your heart?

- Have you wandered from the place of awe and excitement in your relationship with God? What might you do to recover it?

Week 29: Seek Him with All Your Heart

Revelation From the Sacred Place

Week 30

God Knows You

Scripture:

You saw me before I was born. Every day of my life was recorded in your book. Every moment was laid out before a single day had passed.

~ Psalm 139:16 NLT

Reflection Questions:

- When reflecting on how God recorded your life in His book, what springs to mind?

Week 30: God Knows You

- Do you struggle to believe how much God knows you?

- What has God revealed to you through this message?

Week 30: God Knows You

Revelation From the Sacred Place

Week 31

The God Who Sees You

Scripture:

Thereafter, Hagar used another name to refer to the LORD, who had spoken to her. She said, "You are the God who sees me." She also said, "Have I truly seen the One who sees me?"

~ Genesis 16:13 NLT

Reflection Questions:

- Do you know God as El Roi, the God who sees you?

Week 31: The God Who Sees You

- Do you find it easy or difficult to open your heart to God?

- Can you remember the last time God met you somewhere unexpected? What happened?

Week 31: The God Who Sees You

Revelation From the Sacred Place

Week 32

Seasons of Life

Scripture:

For everything there is a season,
a time for every activity under heaven.

~ Ecclesiastes 3:1 NLT

Reflection Questions:

- Does this season feel like a repetitive cycle or is it joyous?

_____

_____

_____

_____

_____

_____

Week 32: Seasons of Life

- Can you recognise what you have learned or what God did during this season?

- How have you managed unexpected seasons in life?

Week 32: Seasons of Life

Revelation From the Sacred Place

Week 33

Favour of the King

Scripture:

When he saw Queen Esther standing there in the inner court, he welcomed her and held out the gold sceptre to her. So Esther approached and touched the end of the sceptre. Then the king asked her, "What do you want, Queen Esther? What is your request? I will give it to you, even if it is half the kingdom!"

~ Esther 5:2-3 NLT

Reflection Questions:

- Think about the King's sceptre pointed towards you. What is your request?

Week 33: Favour of the King

- Have you stepped out in faith even when you felt scared? What happened?

- Can you recall the unexpected blessings given by the King without you asking?

Revelation From the Sacred Place

Week 34

Be Strong and Courageous

Scripture:

This is my command—be strong and courageous! Do not be afraid or discouraged. For the LORD your God is with you wherever you go.

~ Joshua 1:9 NLT

Reflection Questions:

- When greeted with a new challenge or the unexpected, what is your usual response?

Week 34: Be Strong and Courageous

- How do you feel knowing God is with you wherever you are?

- Is anything in your life making you shrink from God's best for you?

Week 34: Be Strong and Courageous

Revelation From the Sacred Place

Week 35

Fear Not

Scripture:

Don't be afraid, for I am with you. Don't be discouraged for I am your God. I will strengthen you and help you. I will hold you up with my victorious right hand.

~ Isaiah 41:10 NLT

Reflection Questions:

- Do you overly worry or have a fearful nature? What is that like for you?

Week 35: Fear Not

- The last time you worried or were fearful, what did it rob you of in your life?

- Can you trust God's loving hands to come through for you?

Revelation From the Sacred Place

Week 36

Confidence in God

Scripture:

And I am certain that God, who began the good work within you, will continue his work until it is finally finished on the day when Christ Jesus returns.

~ Philippians 1:6 NLT

Reflection Questions:

- How does it make you feel, knowing that God will complete the work He has begun in you?

Week 36: Confidence in God

- What conversation might you have with your harsh critic now?

- Do you have the same or more confidence in God?

Revelation From the Sacred Place

Week 37

Keep Going

Scripture:

For I can do everything through Christ, who gives me strength.

~ Philippians 4:13 NLT

Reflection Questions:

- Do you believe you can do all things through Christ who strengthens you?

Week 37: Keep Going

- Do you have a mental picture of your race?

- How does running your race make you feel?

Week 37: Keep Going

Revelation From the Sacred Place

Week 38

Grateful Heart

Scripture:

When the LORD brought back his exiles to Jerusalem, it was like a dream! We were filled with laughter, and we sang for joy. And the other nations said, "What amazing things the LORD has done for them." Yes, the LORD has done amazing things for us! What Joy!

~ Psalm 126:1-3 NLT

Reflection Questions:

- Do you have a song expressing the amazing things God has done for you?

Week 38: Grateful Heart

- Do you have times when you forget? What do you do to remember?

- When God blessed or delivered you, were you able to celebrate?

Week 38: Grateful Heart

Revelation From the Sacred Place

Week 39

Where is Your Trust

Scripture:

But those who trust in the LORD will find new strength. They will soar high on wings like eagles. They will run and not grow weary. They will walk and not faint.

~ Isaiah 40:31 NLT

Reflection Questions:

- Can you recall what your trust was like when it was misplaced?

Week 39: Where is Your Trust

- Do you solely trust in God? If not, what might you do to change this?

- How do you feel knowing God will give you resources when you trust Him?

Week 39: Where is Your Trust

Revelation From the Sacred Place

Week 40

Following Jesus

Scripture:

And now, just as you accepted Christ Jesus as your Lord, you must continue to follow him.

~ Colossians 2:6 NLT

Reflection Questions:

- What was it like for you when you began to follow Jesus?

Week 40: Following Jesus

- Do you have any areas in your life where you need to renew your commitment?

- What has following Jesus cost you? What has following Him gained you?

Week 40: Following Jesus

Revelation From the Sacred Place

Pillar Four:

Purpose

Discover and Fulfill
your God-Given Purpose,
Utilize Giftings Within.

"The Architect's Master Plan."

Week 41

Seek God for the Plan

Scripture:

"For I know the plans I have for you," says the LORD. "They are plans for good and not for disaster, to give you a future and a hope."

~ Jeremiah 29:11 NLT

Reflection Questions:

- How often have you thought about God's plan for your life?

Week 41: Seek God for the Plan

- Do you trust and believe that God has a good plan for you?

- Are you ready to discover and embrace God's plan for your life?

Week 41: Seek God for the Plan

Revelation From the Sacred Place

Week 42

Rahab Believed in the Plan

Scripture:

Meanwhile, Joshua said to the two spies, "Keep your promise. Go to the prostitute's house and bring her out, along with all her family." The men who had been spies went in and brought out Rahab, her father, mother, brothers, and all the other relatives who were with her. They moved her whole family to a safe place near the camp of Israel.

~ Joshua 6:22-23 NLT

Reflection Questions:

- Does your own belief or mindset need an overhaul for the plan?

Week 42: Rahab Believed in the Plan

- Does this story encourage you to find your God-given plan?

Week 42: Rahab Believed in the Plan

Revelation From the Sacred Place

Week 43

Hannah's Need Touched God's Need for the Plan

Scripture:

Hannah was in deep anguish, crying bitterly as she prayed to the LORD. And she made this vow: "O LORD of Heaven's Armies, if you will look upon my sorrow and answer my prayer and give me a son, then I will give him back to you. He will be yours for his entire lifetime, and as a sign that he has been dedicated to the LORD, his hair will never be cut."

~ 1 Samuel 1:10-11 NLT

Reflection Questions:

- Can you give your desires to God and see what He will do?

Week 43: Hannah's Need Touched God's Need for the Plan

- Do you feel you have something ready to birth? Have you talked with God about it?

- Are you accustomed to crying out to God for your needs?

Week 43: Hannah's Need Touched God's Need for the Plan

Revelation From the Sacred Place

Week 44

Leah's Heart of Praise for the Plan

Scripture:

Once again Leah became pregnant and gave birth to another son. She named him Judah, for she said, "Now I will praise the LORD!" And then she stopped having children.

~ Genesis 29:35 NLT

Reflection Questions:

- What parts of Leah's story resonate with you?

Week 44: Leah's Heart of Praise for the Plan

- Can you praise God through your difficult moments? What's that like?

- Will you still trust God with the plan even if it's not what you expect?

Week 44: Leah's Heart of Praise for the Plan

Revelation From the Sacred Place

Week 45

Mary's Agreement for the Plan

Scripture:

Mary asked the angel, "But how can this happen? I am a virgin." The angel replied, "The Holy Spirit will come upon you, and the power of the Most High will overshadow you. So the baby to be born will be holy, and he will be called the Son of God. What's more, your relative Elizabeth has become pregnant in her old age! People used to say she was barren, but she has conceived a son and is now in her sixth month. For the word of God will never fail." Mary responded, "I am the LORD's servant. May everything you have said about me come true." And then the angel left her.

~ Luke 1:34-38 NLT

Reflection Questions:

- Can you say, *"God, let it be as you will for my life?"*

_____

_____

_____

Week 45: Mary's Agreement for the Plan

- What do you think about having a servant's heart like Mary?

- If God gave you an unusual assignment, how quickly would you accept it?

Week 45: Mary's Agreement for the Plan

Revelation From the Sacred Place

Week 46

Naomi and Ruth's Alignment for the Plan

Scripture:

But Ruth replied, "Don't ask me to leave you and turn back. Wherever you go, I will go; wherever you live, I will live. Your people will be my people, and your God will be my God. Wherever you die, I will die, and there I will be buried. May the LORD punish me severely if I allow anything but death to separate us!" When Naomi saw that Ruth was determined to go with her, she said nothing more.

~ Ruth 1:16-18 NLT

Reflection Questions:

- What do you think about Naomi's and Ruth's relationship?

_____

_____

_____

Week 46: Naomi and Ruth's Alignment for the Plan

- How are your relationships in comparison? Can they be improved?

- Do you hope for God to orchestrate something beautiful in your life?

Week 46: Naomi and Ruth's Alignment for the Plan

Revelation From the Sacred Place

Week 47

Jesus Fulfilled the Plan of the Father

Scripture:

"But why did you need to search?" he asked. "Didn't you know I must be in my Father's house?"

~ Luke 2:49 NLT

Reflection Questions:

- What does the will of the Father mean for you?

Week 47: Jesus Fulfilled the Plan of the Father

- What have been notable differences in your life when things just flowed?

- How passionate are you about fulfilling the will of God for your life?

Week 47: Jesus Fulfilled the Plan of the Father

Revelation From the Sacred Place

Week 48

Bearing Lasting Fruit for the Plan

Scripture:

You didn't choose me. I chose you. I appointed you to go and produce lasting fruit, so that the Father will give you whatever you ask for, using my name.

~ John 15:16 NLT

Reflection Questions:

- What are your thoughts on how your lasting fruit will impact others?

Week 48: Bearing Lasting Fruit for the Plan

- Do you see your lasting fruit as an inheritance legacy?

- How do you feel about God choosing you to produce something lasting?

Week 48: Bearing Lasting Fruit for the Plan

Revelation From the Sacred Place

Week 49

God Grants Success

Scripture:

> *Commit your actions to the LORD,*
> *and your plans will succeed.*
>
> ~ Proverbs 16:3 NLT

Reflection Questions:

- Is it easy for you to relinquish your actions to God? If not, what might you do to change this?

Week 49: God Grants Success

- Knowing that God says success is for you, does this encourage you to move forward?

- What areas do you struggle to commit to God? Can you talk with Him about them?

Week 49: God Grants Success

Revelation From the Sacred Place

Week 50

God's Plan for Your Life

Scripture:

The LORD will work out his plans for my life—for your faithful love, O LORD, endures forever. Don't abandon me, for you made me.

~ Psalm 138:8 NLT

Reflection Questions:

- Have you settled in your spirit that God cares and wants your best? If not, what might you do here?

_____

_____

_____

_____

_____

_____

Week 50: God's Plan for Your Life

- Can you share your heart with God?

- Are you able to rest in God's loving assurances for you?

Revelation From the Sacred Place

Week 51

Testify of the Truth

Scripture:

But I will send you the Advocate—the Spirit of truth. He will come to you from the Father and will testify all about me.

~ John 15:26 NLT

Reflection Questions:

- Do you believe the Holy Spirit can empower you to do great things?

Week 51: Testify of the Truth

- How do you feel about the Good News of the Gospel?

- Can you share your faith and the Good News? If not, what prevents this?

Week 51: Testify of the Truth

Revelation From the Sacred Place

Week 52

The Father's Will

Scripture:

Then he said, "Look, I have come to do your will." He cancels the first covenant in order to put the second into effect.

~ Hebrews 10:9 NLT

Revelation From the Sacred Place

Week 52: The Father's Will

Week 52: The Father's Will

About the Author

Josephine Thomas is a devoted wife, loving mother, and committed follower of Christ with a compassionate heart for serving others. Her dedication to ministry and charity work is evident in her unwavering support of widows, orphans, and the broken-hearted. Through her personal journey of navigating complex and painful relationships, Josephine has discovered the profound importance of building and maintaining a deep, significant relationship with God. She speaks from experience, having faced challenges that left scars on her tender spirit. Yet, in the Sacred Place of God's presence, she found healing, restoration, and the affirmation that God will never forsake, undermine, or devalue her. Josephine's testimony is one of triumph, as she learned to trust again and embrace her God-given purpose. Her passion is to see women healed, whole, and aligned with their divine calling—living lives that are fulfilled, joyous, and productive.

For information about group teaching or group coaching, please email: pureandunblemished@gmail.com

Website: www.pureandunblemished.com